THE TRUE STORY OF THE GRANDMOTHER OF JUNETEENTH

OPAL LEE

AND WHAT IT MEANS TO BE FREE

BY
ALICE
FAYE
DUNCAN

ILLUSTRATIONS BY
KETURAH
A. BOBO

Tommy NELSON®

An Imprint of Thomas Nelson
thomasnelson.com

"Happy Juneteenth Jamboree! Come and join the fun!"
Opal Lee waved to her great-grandson as he barreled
across the park.

He zipped past lines of picnic tables covered with
platters of barbecue, baked beans, tomato tarts, and
raspberry cobbler.

HAPPY

He hurried past a leaping choir draped in purple robes. He danced a jig with cowboys playing fiddles, but they did not stop his flow.

Buddy ran to the blooming tree where Opal Lee held court. Her braided hair was a silver crown. Her eyes were twinkling stars.

"Great-Grand Dear!" Buddy called.

"Tell us a Juneteenth story."

Opal Lee raised her face to the sun as
memories of yesteryear filled her vision.

When she had been a Texas bud like the children at her feet, Granddaddy Zack told freedom stories on his wooden porch.

As Opal Lee remembered his words, she lifted her hands and cheered, "Juneteenth means freedom. And now, it's story time!"

Then Opal Lee began . . .

Once upon a blazing sun, Black bodies were bought and sold like cattle.

Black men plowed the fields—but were not allowed to own the land.

Black women cooked the food—but were not allowed to feast on roast and ribs from the master's table.

Black children cleaned the one-room schoolhouses—but were not allowed to read or write.

Earning and learning were against the law. Slavery was a THIEF.

American slavery dragged on like a plague until January 1, 1863. That's when President Lincoln wielded courage and raised his feathered pen. He signed the Emancipation Proclamation with a mighty stroke.

On the 1st day of January, in the year of our Lord one thousand eight hundred and sixty-three, all persons held as slaves ... shall be ... forever free.

Glory! Glory! Glory! Freedom was dazzling news like a bright, starry night.

However, Texas was BIG and many miles away from Mr. Lincoln. White masters defied his words. Black bodies remained in bondage.

They plowed.

They cooked.

They cleaned.

Freedom did not ring through Texas in 1863.

It was toiling times in the Lone Star State. For two years, five months, and eighteen more weary days.

Then, finally, joy jumped up on dancing feet in the gulf town of Galveston.

The year was 1865.

The day was June 19.

Gordon Granger marched through Galveston with Union army troops. The general raised his booming voice and spoke these righteous words:

"The people of Texas are informed that, in accordance with a proclamation from the Executive of the United States, ALL SLAVES ARE FREE."

Opal Lee danced in a circle.

"Freedom, hope, and JOY DIVINE!

Juneteenth means it's FREEDOM TIME!"

Can you imagine the excitement?

Singing filled the air. Happy tears rolled down like rain. Black families leaped through cotton fields and played tambourines.

It was a day of jubilee—perfect for Texas barbecue, watermelon, and sweet potato pie—delicious delights they had been denied during servitude.

Opal Lee told the children, "Remember my words for safekeeping. Remember what I say. Juneteenth is bigger than Texas, singing, or dancing bands. Juneteenth is freedom rising. And freedom is for everyone. Juneteenth is YOU and ME."

As the children clapped and cheered, Buddy tugged her sleeve. "Great-Grand Dear!" he called. "What was Juneteenth like when you were a kid?"

Opal Lee unwrapped another story . . .

Blacks and whites lived separately when I was a child. Jim Crow signs littered old Fort Worth in every public place.

Black families were banned from Forest Park Zoo, except one day of the year. On Juneteenth, we could picnic, party, and ride the Ferris wheel.

I hated that zoo. I loved it too. The birdhouse was my favorite.

Buddy groaned and shook his head.
"The old days don't sound good."

"Good and bad work together like the sun and rain."

I spent good days on my granddaddy's porch
reading poetry books. His farm was my playground.
I ran across the fields and climbed the tallest oak.

"Glory! Glory! Glory! Some memories are
chocolate sweet. But some memories cut and bruise.
My saddest season started on Juneteenth Day, 1939."

An angry mob with flaming sticks
burned my family's brand-new house.
Their broken minds and evil hearts were
so afraid of Black progress. The police
made no arrests. My family moved away.

"And yet the embers burn—that fire still lives in me.

I learned a big lesson that Juneteenth Day. Freedom
is a golden coin. Struggle makes it shine."

"And no matter how long it takes for
freedom to stretch across the land . . .

I will keep on teaching.

I will keep on reaching.

I will keep on walking.

I will keep on talking.

I will raise my voice on the prairie and
the mountaintop until freedom rings."

The children lifted their hands in praise. "Freedom, hope, and JOY DIVINE! Juneteenth means it's FREEDOM TIME!"

Opal Lee winked and chuckled. "I think now it's time for barbecue, strawberry cake, and red Juneteenth punch."

"Glory! Glory! Glory!" Buddy cheered and waved his hands. When he bounced up to leave, Opal Lee hugged him tightly.

Then, just like birds in flight, all the children flocked into her arms. Opal Lee studied their shining faces.

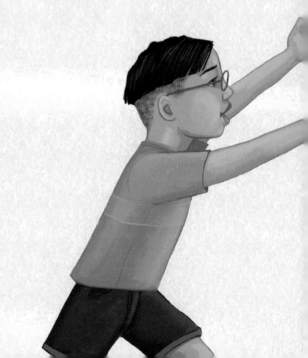

BLACK

BROWN

BRONZE

GOLD

TAN WHITE

FRECKLES!

As the children dashed away, she
marveled at the bright future.

She rested against the blooming tree and whispered into the wind: "Remember my words for safekeeping. Remember what I say. Freedom is for everyone. Juneteenth is YOU and ME."

JUNETEENTH "RED PUNCH" STRAWBERRY LEMONADE

In Texas, Big Red is a bottled soft drink also called "red soda water." The red cream soda is often served at Juneteenth celebrations. This punch recipe is easy to make and offers a new, puckering and pleasing twist to the traditional red soda water that has been made in Texas since 1937.

Ingredients

2 cups fresh strawberries, stems and leaves removed
    or 2 cups thawed frozen strawberries
½ cup sugar
1 12-ounce can lemonade concentrate, thawed
    or 1 cup fresh-squeezed lemon juice (about 8 lemons)
7 cups cold water

Instructions

1. Slice the strawberries.
2. Place the ingredients in a blender in order. (If you don't have a blender, place the ingredients in a large mixing bowl, and use a hand mixer on low speed to combine the punch until smooth.)
3. Pulse the mixture a few times. Then blend at low speed for 2 minutes.
4. Gradually turn the speed up to medium. Blend until smooth.
5. Pour into a large pitcher or punch bowl. Serve over ice.

Makes 10 servings

Recipe courtesy of Angela Shelf Medearis, author of *The New African-American Kitchen*, *The Kitchen Diva Cooks!*, and *The Kitchen Diva's Diabetic Cookbook*.

JUNETEENTH TIMELINE

1619—Twenty captured Africans arrive in Jamestown, Virginia. They are the first Africans sold into slavery in the British North American colonies.

JULY 4, 1776—Congress adopts the Declaration of Independence, announcing the colonies' separation from Great Britain. The liberties given in this document are not extended to enslaved people.

SEPTEMBER 22, 1862—During the Civil War, President Abraham Lincoln announces the Emancipation Proclamation. It sets January 1, 1863, as the date of freedom for over three million people living as slaves. His document establishes that the Civil War is a fight against slavery.

JANUARY 1, 1863—President Abraham Lincoln officially signs the Emancipation Proclamation, releasing Black servants from bondage in the Confederacy. Many Black men volunteer to join the Union army and help win the war.

APRIL 9, 1865—Confederate General Robert E. Lee surrenders to Union General Ulysses S. Grant at Appomattox Court House in Virginia. This event ends the Civil War.

JUNE 19, 1865—Over two years after Lincoln's signing of the Emancipation Proclamation, General Gordon Granger reads "General Order No. 3" in Galveston and ends slavery in Texas. This day is now called Juneteenth.

DECEMBER 6, 1865—The Thirteenth Amendment is ratified when three-fourths of the states approve it. The amendment makes slavery illegal in America.

JUNE 19, 1866—The first official Juneteenth celebrations take place in Galveston and other Texas towns and cities. The celebrations grow across the nation in the following years as free Blacks migrate beyond the American South.

JUNE 1968—During the Poor People's Campaign in Washington, DC, civil rights leader Ralph Abernathy encourages Black Americans to rededicate themselves to celebrating Juneteenth as they pursue economic and civil rights following the assassination of Dr. Martin Luther King Jr.

JANUARY 1, 1980—Juneteenth becomes an official state holiday in Texas.

2020—By this time, forty-seven American states celebrate Juneteenth as a state holiday or day of observance.

JUNE 15, 2021—The US Senate and Congress vote to make Juneteenth a national holiday commemorating the end of American slavery. President Joe Biden signs the legislation into law with Grandmother Opal Lee standing at his side.

OPAL LEE: THE GRANDMOTHER OF JUNETEENTH

Opal Lee is a story keeper and historian. She says, "If we don't remember what we have been through, our nation is doomed to repeat it."

Opal was born in Marshall, Texas, on October 7, 1926, but she grew up in Fort Worth. Her grandfather, Zachrah Broadous Sr., was the son of an enslaved mother. Opal learned from her "Papa" how President Lincoln ended slavery in the southern Confederate states with the signing of the Emancipation Proclamation on January 1, 1863. But Texas was large, remote, and without protection from Union troops. So the enslaved people there did not receive the news of their freedom until over two years later. Finally, on June 19, 1865, General Gordon Granger arrived in Galveston and served Lincoln's order to free the enslaved. This day of freedom is called *Juneteenth*, a word that combines *June* and *nineteenth*.

The first Juneteenth anniversary was celebrated in Texas on June 19, 1866. Black Americans gathered in clearings to feast on vibrant red foods they were denied during servitude, such as barbecue, strawberry pie, and punch made with fresh fruit. They gathered to remember the sorrow of enslavement as well as to sing and celebrate the joy of liberation. At least seven freedoms were gained for Black Americans following Juneteenth and the Thirteenth Amendment to the US Constitution in 1865. Blacks could now (1) work for wages, (2) own land, (3) name themselves, (4) read and write, (5) serve in the military, (6) travel, and (7) worship freely.

Called the "Grandmother of Juneteenth," Opal Lee led a movement to make Juneteenth a national holiday. From 2016 to 2020, she walked across America and collected more than 1.5 million signatures for her petition to the US Congress. It was a journey complete with rejection and disappointments. Nothing stopped her. Opal continued her walk. And when she was ninety-four years old, President Joe Biden signed legislation to make Juneteenth a national holiday commemorating the end of American slavery.

Opal Lee's constant reminder is wise advice: "None of us are free until we're all free, and we aren't free yet."

SOURCES

Carmel, Julia. "Opal Lee's Juneteenth Vision Is Becoming Reality." *New York Times*, June 18, 2020. https://www.nytimes.com/2020/06/18/style/opal-lee-juneteenth.html.

Conner, Robert C. *General Gordon Granger: The Savior of Chickamauga and the Man Behind "Juneteenth."* Philadelphia: Casemate, 2013.

Davis, Michael. "National Archives Safeguards Original 'Juneteenth' General Order." *National Archives News*, June 19, 2020. https://www.archives.gov/news/articles/juneteenth-original-document.

"The Emancipation Proclamation." *National Archives*. https://www.archives.gov/exhibits/featured-documents/emancipation-proclamation.

"Juneteenth '83: Blacks Remember Past, Plan Future." *Fort Worth Star-Telegram*, June 19, 1983, 19.

Kojo Nnamdi Show. "Honoring Juneteenth: Food as a Form of Celebration." Produced by Kayla Hewitt. WAMU 88.5, June 17, 2020. MP3 audio. https://wamu.org/story/20/06/17/honoring-juneteenth-food-as-a-form-of-celebration/.

Lee, Opal. Phone interview with author, December 10, 2020.

Nelson, Vaunda Micheaux, Drew Nelson, and Mark Schroder. *Juneteenth*. 2006. Reprint, Minneapolis: Millbrook Press, 2020.

Penk, Walt. "Family Tradition Important: This Black Family Has Roots Too." *Statesman Journal* (Salem, OR), May 2, 1977, 3.

Sims, Dione. Phone interview with author, July 10, 2020.

Sims, Dione. Phone interview with author, September 30, 2020.

Smith, Diane. "Fort Worth's Opal Lee Has Step-by-Step Plan to Highlight Juneteenth." *Fort Worth Star-Telegram*, August 31, 2016. https://www.star-telegram.com/news/local/fort-worth/article99107727.html.

Thomas, Karen M. "Juneteenth Remembers Slavery, Celebrates Freedom." *Chicago Tribune*, June 18, 1992. https://www.chicagotribune.com/news/ct-xpm-1992-06-18-9202230965-story.html.

"Violence Flares, Then Is Quelled." *Fort Worth Star-Telegram*, June 20, 1939, 1.

In memory of

Mary Alice Lee

Owens Walsh

—A.F.D.

To Cora Lee

Ogden and

Lucinda Hayes

—K.A.B.

Library of Congress Cataloging-in-Publication Data

Library of Congress Cataloging-in-Publication Data
Names: Duncan, Alice Faye, author. | Bobo, Keturah A., illustrator.
Title: Opal Lee and what it means to be free : the true story of the grandmother of Juneteenth / by Alice Faye Duncan ; illustrations by Keturah A Bobo.
Other titles: True story of the grandmother of Juneteenth
Description: Nashville, Tennessee : Thomas Nelson, [2022] | Includes bibliographical references. | Audience: Ages 4-8 | Summary: "The true story of Black activist Opal Lee and her vision of Juneteenth as a holiday for everyone will inspire children to be brave and make a difference. Growing up in Texas, Opal knew the history of Juneteenth, but she soon discovered that most Americans had never heard of the holiday that represents the nation's creed of "freedom for all.""-- Provided by publisher.
Identifiers: LCCN 2021021196 (print) | LCCN 2021021197 (ebook) | ISBN 9781400231256 (hardcover) | ISBN 9781400231270 (epub)
Subjects: LCSH: Lee, Opal, 1926- | Juneteenth--Juvenile literature. | African American women civil rights workers--Texas--Juvenile literature. | African Americans--Anniversaries, etc.--Juvenile literature. | Slaves--Emancipation--Texas--Juvenile literature. | African Americans--Social life and customs--Juvenile literature. | African Americans--Texas--History--Juvenile literature. | BISAC: JUVENILE NONFICTION / Biography & Autobiography / Social Activists | JUVENILE NONFICTION / Holidays & Celebrations / Patriotic Holidays
Classification: LCC E185.93.T4 D86 2021 (print) | LCC E185.93.T4 (ebook) | DDC 323.092 [B]--dc23
LC record available at https://lccn.loc.gov/2021021196
LC ebook record available at https://lccn.loc.gov/2021021197

Printed in Korea

22 23 24 25 26 SAM 10 9 8 7 6 5 4 3 2 1

Mfr: SAM / Samhwa, Korea / January 2022 / PO #12055663